MW01148771

DATE DUE

Demco, Inc. 38-293

TOY LAB

Michael Elsohn Ross
with illustrations by Tim Seeley

Valley Christian Junior High School
P.O. Box 18820
San Jose, CA 95158

✌ Carolrhoda Books, Inc./Minneapolis

To Carl Brownless,
for allowing me to experiment with your kids
—M.E.R.

Each experiment described in this book is intended solely for the purpose of illustrating the scientific principles and concepts identified with that experiment. The experiments should not be performed in any manner or for any purpose other than as described herein. The experiments should not be performed in any manner or for any purpose loss sustained, directly or indirectly, as a result of the application or use of any experiment for any other purpose, or the performance of any experiment other than in strict accordance with the instructions contained herein.

Text copyright © 2003 by Michael Elsohn Ross
Illustrations copyright © 2003 by Carolrhoda Books, Inc.

All rights reserved. International copyright secured. No part of this book may be reproduced, stored in a retrieval system, or transmitted in any form or by any means— electronic, mechanical, photocopying, recording, or otherwise—without the prior written permission of Carolrhoda Books, Inc., except for brief quotations in an acknowledged review.

Carolrhoda Books, Inc.
A division of Lerner Publishing Group
241 First Avenue North, Minneapolis, MN 55401 U.S.A.

Website address: www.lernerbooks.com

Library of Congress Cataloging-in-Publication Data

Ross, Michael Elsohn, 1952–
    Toy lab / by Michael Elsohn Ross ; illustrations by Tim Seeley.
    p.   cm. — (You are the scientist)
    Includes index.
    Summary: Explains how to do experiments related
to various scientific principles using different kinds of toys.
    ISBN: 0–87614–456–3 (lib. bdg. : alk. paper)
    1. Physics—Experiments—Juvenile literature.
    [1. Toys—Experiments. 2. Science—Experiments.
    3. Experiments.] I. Seeley, Tim, ill. II. Title.
    QC26 .R67 2003
    530'.078—dc21   2001005456

Manufactured in the United States of America
1 2 3 4 5 6 – JR – 08 07 06 05 04 03

TABLE OF CONTENTS

WANTED:
Kids to play with toys!

Imagine being an employee at a toy research center. All day long, you could mess around with toys and share your discoveries. You might devise experiments with yo-yos or test new designs for boats. You could compare the power of squirt guns or the burps of burping dolls. As you conducted experiment after experiment, secrets of the universe might come to light. Without even intending to, you could find yourself exploring big ideas like gravity or flight. No one would say, "Hey, quit playing and get to work. Do the dishes. Clean up your room. Finish your homework." They would know that you were doing the most important work of kids—just playing.

Unfortunately, you aren't being offered a position at a toy research center, but you *are* invited to start a research center of your own. Most kids are toy scientists without even knowing it. Scientific experiments grow from questions, comparisons, challenges, or problems. Whenever you start to explore how toys work or what they can do, or create experiments with them, you are knocking at the doorways to scientific mysteries.

YOUR LABORATORY

Anywhere at all can be a toy research lab. Of course, sometimes you may find yourself playing in the wrong place at the wrong time. Here are some basic tips to make your toy studies go more smoothly:

▶ Ask permission before you use other kids' toys or other people's materials. (For example, make sure it's OK before you convert the living room into a test site for launching toys into space.)

▶ Consider how the experiment might affect your toys. Think before you do something that might damage them.

▶ **Forget about** any tests with fire, electricity, or anything else dangerous, unless you are supervised by a responsible adult.

▶ When you have an experiment in progress, alert other members of your household. Perhaps you can make a sign that states there is an important toy experiment in action!

▶ To tune your parents in to the importance of toy science, show them this article from the fictional newspaper column "Popular Scientists."

TOYS LEAD TO SUCCESS

Stockholm, Sweden: Today Doctor Rosie Nastasi was awarded the Nobel Prize in physics for her pioneering work in the field of cosmology. Her discoveries have led to new theories about the origins of the universe and add immensely to the work of Hubble, Einstein, and other twentieth-century physicists. When asked about her reasons for exploring the complexities of the universe, Dr. Nastasi replied, "It all started with toys. My room was always a mess. I was constantly experimenting with Lego blocks, squirt guns, dolls, and weird stuff like Silly Putty. My folks just closed the door and left me alone. I never did crazy stuff like blow up Barbie dolls or anything, but I did test the limits of remote-control cars and other mechanical gadgets. Before long, I was wondering not only how toys work, but how the whole universe operates."

After an impressive early career that includes teaching at M.I.T. and research at the National Space Center, Dr. Nastasi says she has only begun to explore. "It's like playing with toys—you never want to quit, even when it's dinner time." When asked to give advice to today's junior scientists, she simply says, "Play, and question everything!"

GUINEA PIG MAN NABS CR

Guinea Pig Man at the scene of an attempted toy store robbe
yesterday afternoon. Pictured are Late Knight, Pondhead, F

QUESTIONS EVERYWHERE Some folks are constantly asking questions. How does a Slinky work? Why do spinning tops fall over when they slow down? How does a paper airplane fly? People who question the world around them may find themselves on the path of scientific exploration. Like other curious explorers who have come before, they don't know where they are headed, but they have a reason to get started. Experiments grow from questions. Listen to your questions and let them push you into adventure!

Here are some questions from kids at El Portal Elementary School:

► What's the best kind of stairs to make a Slinky walk down—carpeted, wood, or concrete?
► What makes a boomerang come back?
► Will a big Frisbee glide farther than a small one?
► Do magnetic marbles work underwater?
► Why do some balls bounce higher than others do?
► Will a water balloon pop in hot water?
► How does wind affect the shooting range of a squirt gun?

WHAT IF . . .

When you follow your questions, they lead to tests. What if I tied a rock to my action figure? Would it sink? What if I threw a Frisbee from a high place, like the top of a slide? Would it fly farther?

As you play with your toys, pay attention to these "what if" questions. Design tests to find out what happens. Here are guidelines for your tests:

▶ Use fair tests. For example, if you are testing to see which one of two balls bounces higher, both balls should be dropped from the same exact height in the same place to be fair. It definitely wouldn't be a fair test if one ball was thrown down hard and the other was just dropped, would it?

▶ Perform your test several times to see if the same thing happens every time.

▶ Record what happens by taking notes, pictures, or video footage.

▶ Share your results with friends and family, and challenge them to repeat your tests to see if they get the same results.

TO THE DRAWING BOARD Some tests lead to new designs. Could you design a toy car that would go faster or a parachute that would stay aloft longer? Have you ever considered redesigning your toys to see if you could make them work differently? Like a creator of racing cars or rockets, you can make changes in your toys to see if they might work better.

▶ Choose one part of the toy to change at a time. That way you will know what effect the change has on how your toy works. If you change too many things at once, you will be clueless about which change made the toy behave differently.

▶ Repeat your test several times to see if the design change makes the toy act the same way each time.

▶ Make a new toy based on the changes. Perhaps you'll have a winner at the next science fair or invention contest.

THE SCIENTIFIC METHOD

The scientific method is like a recipe for discovery. As you explore your toys, try the following recipe and see what you cook up!

1. Start with a question or guess. (For example: "I think magnetic marbles will come together in water.") Write it down. Keep a lab notebook.
2. Test. (For example: Put two marbles in a tub of water 6 centimeters apart from each other and watch to see if they come together. Compare it with putting the marbles 6 centimeters apart on a wood floor.) Record your results.
3. Repeat. Repeat. Repeat! Do your test several times under the same conditions to see if the same things happen. Write down what happens each time so you can compare.
4. Draw a conclusion. Why do you think you got the results you did? Jot down your ideas.
5. Modify and retest. If you feel like it, you can change the test slightly and do it over. (For example: Put the marbles in a tub of water 9 centimeters apart and watch them to see what happens.) Remember to change only one part of your test at a time, so the results are clear.

As you play with toys, any experiment that you come up with will help you learn something new. That's the great thing about experiments. Whether they deliver the answer you were looking for or not, you always end up with something, even if it's another mystery.

WEIRD STUFF AND
STRANGE SUBSTANCES

Like most kids, you've probably been told not to play with your food. Food is not considered a toy by grown-ups, but anything that is fun to play with, whether it comes from a toy store or not, works for kids. During the last 50 years, toy makers have realized that weird substances make great toys. They also make great tools for exploring the properties of matter, the stuff that things are made of. As you play with strange substances, whether Silly Putty or gloop, you might find yourself bumping into big ideas about little stuff.

Here's a short list of some toys you could use for research into the properties of matter:

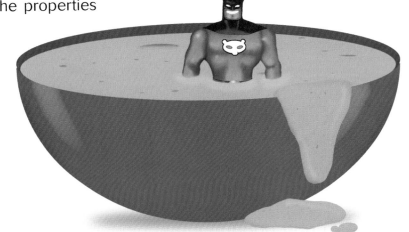

- ► bubbles
- ► gloop
- ► Icky Poo
- ► Play-Doh
- ► Silly Putty

HOW TO MAKE GLOOP

SUPPLIES

borax (cleaning agent)	metric measuring cup
white glue	wooden spoon
3 teacups or mugs	metric measuring spoon
1 large bowl	water

1. In the large bowl, mix together 125 ml of water with 500 ml of glue.
2. In each teacup, pour 80 ml of warm water.
3. Stir 5 ml of borax into the water in each cup.
4. Add one teacup of the borax-and-water mixture to the glue mixture in the large bowl. Mix it in with the wooden spoon.
5. Add the next cup of the borax mixture to the large bowl. Mix, and add the last cup. The gloop will get stringy. Keep mixing with your hands until all the water is mixed in.
6. Store gloop in a plastic container with a tight-fitting lid.

What's the Big Idea?

MATTER Everything that takes up space—whether it is a solid, a liquid, or a gas—is called matter. Whatever matter is made of, it has distinct qualities that we can discover as we interact with it. Our senses enable us to analyze the characteristics of matter that we encounter in our daily lives, whether the matter is in the form of a pile of mud or a bowl of cereal. Certain toys, such as Silly Putty or gloop, have characteristics that are very different from everyday matter. These toys are fun to explore. Playing with them reveals their weird properties. Like a scientist exploring matter in a new universe, you can test your ideas about what these strange play substances can and can't do.

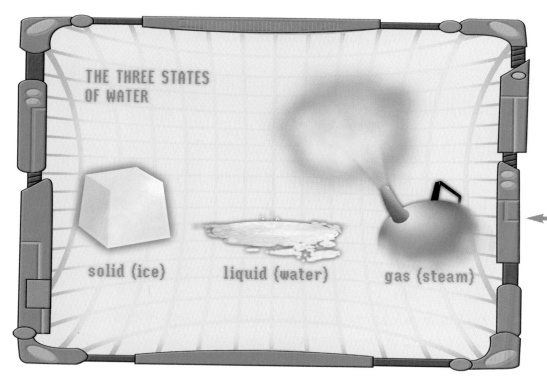

THE THREE STATES OF WATER

solid (ice)   liquid (water)   gas (steam)

KIDExperiments

QUESTIONING GLOOP Ali and Nicole had all sorts of gloopy questions and decided to answer some of them through simple tests.

► Will gloop regroup?

Ali dropped separate bits of gloop on her desk and waited to see if they came together. The pieces were not touching when they landed. She waited and waited, but the gloop didn't regroup. Ali decided that the pieces wouldn't rejoin each other.

► Will gloop spit out a marble?

The girls noticed that gloop was springy, like bread dough. If you put something in it, would it spring back out? When they poked marbles into a glob of gloop, the gloop slowly pushed them back out.

► Will dropped gloop break?

Nicole dropped handfuls of gloop from an arm's length above the gloop container. Splat! When the gloop hit, it split! This happened even from a height of just a few centimeters.

PUTTY PLAY After Nick had spent a few hours goofing around with some Silly Putty, he had some ideas about what it could and couldn't do. For example, he noticed that when he folded it over onto itself and squeezed, it made cool popping sounds. He also discovered that when it was pulled softly and slowly it stretched, but it broke when it was pulled hard and fast.

It seemed to him that when the Silly Putty was molded into a hollow ball, it bounced better than when it was solid. To find out for sure, he set up a test with two balls of putty. One was hollow and one solid, but both were about the same size. Nick dropped each from a height of 1 meter and recorded how high each bounced. Here are his results:

	HOLLOW BALL	SOLID BALL
test 1	10 cm	41 cm
test 2	23 cm	48 cm
test 3	28 cm	61 cm
test 4	28 cm	51 cm
test 5	30 cm	53 cm

As you can see, the solid ball bounced higher. Do you have any ideas why? Nick thought that it bounced higher because it was heavier. Do all solid balls bounce higher than hollow balls of the same size and the same material? You might want to check it out.

HISTORY OF SILLY PUTTY

What do you do with a new substance that doesn't work the way you want it to? Why not turn it into a toy? During World War II, the United States military needed a cheap substitute for rubber. An engineer named James Wright at General Electric Company was assigned the job of coming up with an inexpensive rubberlike substance that could be used for everything from tires to gas masks.

Wright did indeed create something new. It stretched more than rubber and bounced better. It didn't break down in heat or cold, and it did weird things like lifting ink off a newspaper. Unfortunately, it didn't work out as a rubber substitute, but it did make a great toy.

Though engineers tried to figure out a good use for the stuff, which they called "nutty putty," it was a toy store owner named Paul Hodgson who realized it was pretty cool to play with. He packaged it in plastic eggs and named it Silly Putty. Silly Putty was a hit and soon became a favorite toy throughout the world.

FLYING DISKS
AND SOARING PEAS

Toys that fly and toys that send objects soaring into the air are gateways to exploring basic principles of flight. As you goof around with flight, whether it's catapulting peas at the dinner table (just joking) or testing a new glider, question what you see. Perhaps you want to compare the flying abilities of a whole array of flying toys and objects. Just remember that flight experiments have their appropriate time and place. Rather than testing a Frisbee inside, where it might exit through a plate glass window, choose a research area that will keep you out of trouble. Hint: Peas are best catapulted in the backyard, unless you want to miss dessert!

Here's a short list of some toys you could use for flight research:

- balloon
- balsa glider
- boomerang
- catapult
- Frisbee
- kite

- Koosh Woosh
- paper glider
- parachute
- rocket
- windup plane

How to Make a Parachute

SUPPLIES

square of cloth (bandanna or hankie)	action figures
four 30-cm lengths of string or yarn	large washers
large paper clip	

1. Tie a string to each corner of the cloth.

2. Attach the free ends of the strings to the paper clip.

3. Pry out part of the paper clip to make a hook.

4. Attach a washer or an action figure to the paper clip, ball the parachute up in your hand, and toss it high into the air.

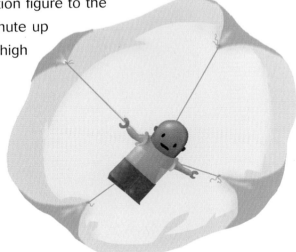

What's the Big Idea?

FLIGHT Bird wings, airplane wings, and Frisbees all have airfoils to allow them to fly. An airfoil is a surface that is curved more above than below. Air moves along a wing's upper surface at a higher speed than it moves along the underside. According to a scientific law called Bernoulli's principle, the faster a gas or fluid travels, the less pressure it exerts. So the upper surface of the wing has less pressure exerted on it than the underside. This difference in air pressure causes the wing to rise when it is moved forward through the air. This upward force is called lift, and it is what allows Frisbees and toy gliders to rise toward the heavens.

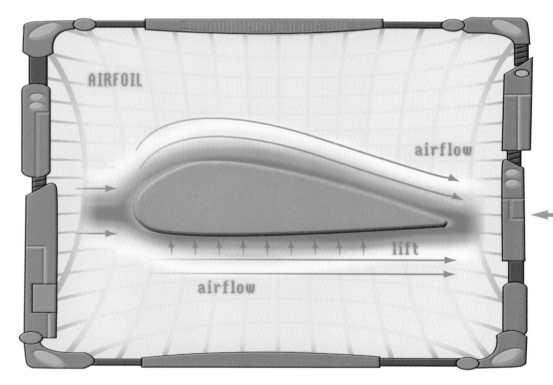

AIRFOIL

airflow

lift

airflow

KID Experiments

EXCESS BAGGAGE How does the added weight of paper clips affect the flight of a toy plane? Aron and Rhyen conducted some tests to see if they could improve the flight of a store-bought Styrofoam plane. Without any added weight, the plane did a perfect glide and flew a distance of 5.4 meters. Adding a paper clip to the nose caused the plane to dive, and it went only 3 meters. When they removed the paper clip from the nose and put one on the tip of each wing, the plane flew higher but dropped faster. It covered a distance of only 3.9 meters. Next, they took the clips off the wings and put one on the tail end. When they tossed the plane into the air, it made a flip and then dove to the ground, covering a distance of only 3.6 meters. Aron and Rhyen figured the plane had been designed well to begin with and had just the right weight on the nose.

BIG DISK, LITTLE DISK Will a big Frisbee fly farther than a smaller one? Equipped with a measuring tape and two Frisbees, Leanne, Allison, Elizabeth, Katelyn, and Melissa took turns tossing the Frisbees and measuring the distances that they flew. Here are their results:

	BIG FRISBEE	LITTLE FRISBEE
test 1	41 m	22 m
test 2	72 m	73 m
test 3	99 m	23 m
test 4	23 m	19 m

As the girls tried to analyze the differences in the distances covered by the whizzing disks, they realized that the length of flights varied because of how each person threw the Frisbees. Some threw them harder. Some messed up when they tossed them, so that the Frisbees dove to the ground. The girls thought that maybe just one person should throw the Frisbees and that only the good throws should be counted. You could repeat their test and see what you discover.

HISTORY OF THE
FRISBEE

During the 1950s, people were fascinated by the idea of flying saucers arriving from outer space. An inventor named Walter Frederick Morrison decided to make a toy that not only looked like a flying saucer but flew like one too. His first flying disk was made of lightweight metal. In 1957 Wham-O Company of southern California produced his disks in plastic and dubbed them "Flyin' Saucers." Soon they were whizzing about all over sunny California beaches. On a promotional tour to colleges on the East Coast, Wham-O's president, Richard Knerr, saw students at Yale University playing a game that involved tossing metal pie tins. The tins were from the Frisbie Pie Company, so the students called them "frisbies." Knerr liked the name and renamed his plastic disk the Frisbee. It wasn't long before Frisbee was a household word and a national craze.

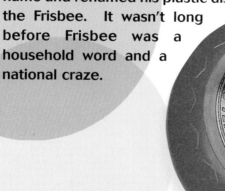

THE FLIGHT OF THE FRISBEE

Have you ever been frustrated by trying to keep a Frisbee flying on the level? Instead of soaring in a nice long flight, the disk dives, hits the ground, and rolls on its rim. Rather than releasing the disk in a horizontal position, more experienced throwers have learned to adjust the angle. A disk can be tilted slightly as it's thrown to compensate for the varying lift of the disk. Engineers call this process "adjusting the hyzer angle." For example, if you use a clockwise spin, release the disk with the left side tilted down. This will counteract the tendency of the spin to tilt the disk to the right and make it flop over.

Another odd behavior of flying disks is when they change direction of flight and come flying right back at you like a boomerang. This is great if you are trying to play catch by yourself, but it doesn't help if

you are tossing a disk to a friend. This action is called "the turnover effect." Many styles of flying disks have been designed, but all exhibit the turnover effect.

In the early 1980s, a Swiss student named Macé Schuurmans wondered about the turnover effect. He wrote a paper about the turnover effect and how it might be eliminated. His paper earned him a place in the second round of a science competition, and one of the judges even offered him the use of a lab. Experimenting with a special tank, Macé suspended a spinning disk in water and released ink to see the patterns of flow around the disk. Instead of finding a way to eliminate the turnover effect, he discovered that the flow is complex and unpredictable. Things were not as simple as he had hoped.

Frisbees and other flying disks are only partially understood, but you don't have to know everything about a flying disk to be a champion thrower. Macé's long hours of flight tests paid off. He became a Swiss national disk-throwing champion and has toured on the national team.

LITTLE SQUIRTS
AND BIG WAVES

Messing around with water and water toys can spill into discoveries about the properties of liquids. While you bathe in the tub or cool off in a water fight, you might find yourself exploring waves or water pressure without intending to. You might even wonder about waves as you hop over a jump rope or play with a Slinky or another wavy material. As you get into wild explorations with water, consider where you set up your lab. The bathtub or backyard might be a better location than your parent's bedroom!

got hot?
get cool!

water
only 25¢

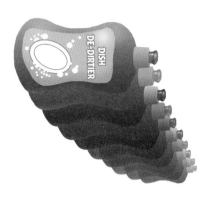 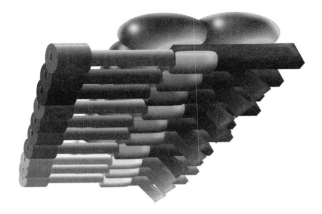

Here's a short list of some toys you could use for research on the properties of liquids:

- ▶ boat
- ▶ jump rope
- ▶ Slinky
- ▶ squirt gun

- ▶ Super Soaker
- ▶ water balloon
- ▶ water rocket

HOW TO MAKE SQUIRTERS

SUPPLIES

window cleaner bottle (rinsed)	water balloons
dish detergent bottle (rinsed)	rubber bands
old eyedroppers or medicine droppers	plastic tubing

Squirters can be made from all sorts of plastic containers. Most are free or inexpensive. Be sure to clean old containers well before using. Invent your own squirter with rubber bands and plastic tubing or containers you find around the house.

Valley Christian Junior High School
P.O. Box 18820
San Jose, CA 95158

What's the Big Idea?

PRESSURE Did you know that squirt guns are mini-pumps? As you squeeze the gun's trigger, water is pushed up through the tubing and out of the nozzle of the gun. Since the hole at the nozzle is small, water is forced out in a pressurized stream. This causes the water to shoot out of the gun. Have you ever played around with shooting water from a hose or even your mouth? The smaller you make the exit hole, the more pressure you produce and the farther you can send the water. No doubt you'll find some good excuses to experiment with water pressure on a hot summer day.

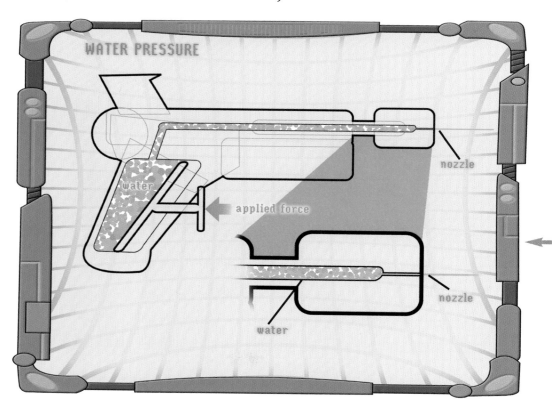

WATER PRESSURE

nozzle

water

applied force

nozzle

water

WAVES Waves begin with the disturbance of an object. A pebble dropped into a pool of water causes small waves to travel outward from the place where the pebble disturbed the surface. Cracking a whip causes waves to travel along the whip.

With a large spring like a Slinky, you can see several types of waves. When a Slinky or a jump rope is stretched between two people, one person can create waves by moving his end up and down. These waves, which move toward the other person, are called transverse waves. A transverse wave's movement is perpendicular to the source of movement.

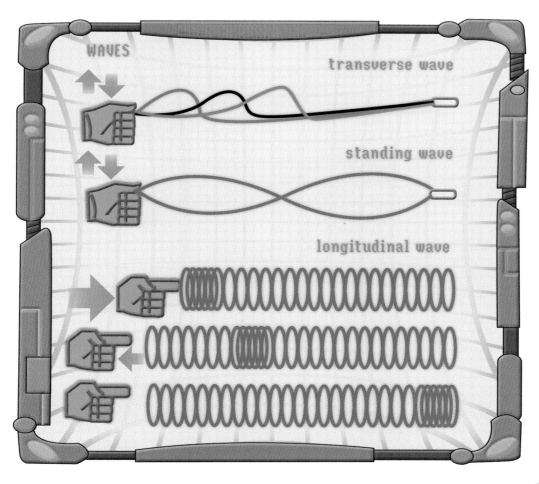

T 20904

If one end of the Slinky or jump rope is moved back and forth at a constant speed, the waves will appear to stand still. As the waves traveling outward from the person moving the Slinky meet the waves coming back from the other end, a standing wave is created. A standing wave is a special kind of transverse wave.

A longitudinal wave moves parallel to the original movement. If one of the people holding the Slinky pulls her end toward her and then pushes it away from her, she'll send a longitudinal wave down the Slinky. A pulse of coils will travel down the Slinky and back.

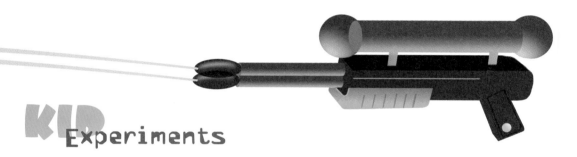

KID Experiments

BIG SQUIRT Here's some important research that could help you in your next squirt gun fight!

One blustery day, Kyle was getting annoyed by the wind as he was testing to see how far his squirt gun could shoot. Rico suggested that they use the wind as part of their test. The boys shot into the wind, with the wind, and when there was no wind. They thought the gun would shoot the farthest when shot with the wind. Here are their results:

WITH WIND		AGAINST WIND		NO WIND	
test 1	6.25 meters	test 1	5 meters	test 1	3.23 meters
test 2	8.28 meters	test 2	5 meters	test 2	2 meters
test 3	8 meters	test 3	5.26 meters	test 3	4.31 meters

They had thought that the water would squirt the farthest when it was being blown by the wind, and they were right. But the water squirted farther against the wind than when there was no wind. Why do you think that happened? Try it out and see if you get similar results.

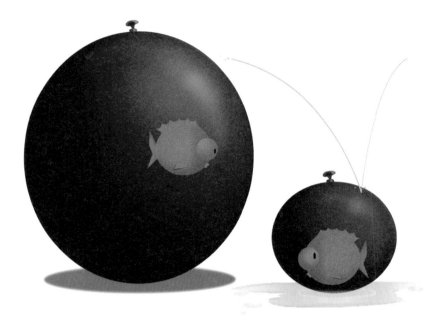

THE BEST BALLOONS Have you ever wondered how to make the most explosive water balloons? Brittany, Candice, and Nalani filled up water balloons with different amounts of water. They tested the water balloons by dropping them onto the ground from heights of 6 and 8 feet. They also tested the balloons by throwing them at some boys who were getting nosy about their experiments. The more water in the balloon, they discovered, the more easily it broke. When they put just a small amount of water in a balloon, it bounced like a ball. Nalani thought that the more water a balloon holds, the thinner its skin becomes and the more easily it breaks. Do you agree? You could test her ideas on your friends.

PRESSURE'S ON   Nicole tested a variety of substances to see which would shoot the farthest from a squirt gun. Here are her results:

milk	6.30 meters
saltwater	5.73 meters
sugar water	5.06 meters
plain water	5.01 meters

Why do you think the milk went the farthest? Do you think it would go the farthest on every test? Nicole thought it outdistanced the others because it is lighter. Do you agree?

Though the Slinky seems to be a perfect toy, it wasn't invented for play. During World War II, an engineer named Richard James was experimenting with springs that would keep a ship's instruments working when the ship was rocking back and forth in rough ocean waves. James couldn't get his original idea to work, but when he accidentally knocked one of his springs off a shelf, he noticed it behaved rather strangely. Like a slithery snake, it climbed down from the shelf, to a stack of books, to the tabletop. He tried the spring on the stairs and found out how well it walked downstairs. His wife realized that Richard had invented a great toy. She fished for a good name in the dictionary and came up with "Slinky"!

The Jameses started making the Slinky for kids. Ever since, these long, lanky springs have been a hit. Clever adults have figured out some non-play uses. During the Vietnam War, soldiers tossed Slinkies into trees to make outdoor radio antennas. Some farmers use a Slinky-like spring in a machine that picks pecans. The Slinky has even gone into space. Can you imagine a Slinky in zero gravity? It doesn't act springy or end up in a nice little pile. It just waves around like a happily wiggling snake.

TOWERS, BRIDGES, AND RAMPS

splat!

Have you ever noticed a baby dropping things from his high chair? Kids start exploring gravity from the very start. That doesn't mean, however, that you are too old to learn more. Construction toys enable us both to build cool structures and to add to the construction of new ideas about gravity. As you build things that stand up, fall down, or break apart, you might just find yourself falling into some new understandings.

Here's a short list of some toys you could use for gravity and construction research:

- ► balls
- ► Erector set
- ► Hot Wheels tracks
- ► Kapla Building Planks
- ► Lego blocks
- ► Lincoln Logs

- ► marbles
- ► Mega Bloks
- ► playing cards
- ► Tinkertoys
- ► toy cars
- ► wooden blocks

HOW TO MAKE RACING CAR RAMPS

SUPPLIES

one pack of foam pipe insulation	plastic containers
blocks	sharp knife
toy racing cars	marbles

1. Ask an adult to help you slice the foam tubes in half lengthwise. (One side will be scored to begin with.)
2. The cupped halves of the tube are ramps. Support the ramps with blocks or plastic containers to make inclines of varying steepness.
3. Send marbles or cars down your ramps for a ride.

GO GO GRAVITY!

These flexible ramps can be bent, twisted, and combined to make wild and wacky highways for toy cars or marbles.

What's the Big Idea?

GRAVITY Gravity is the force of attraction that acts between all objects in the universe because of their mass. Unlike magnetic energy, which can attract or repel, gravity is only attractive. Large, massive objects, such as our planet, attract smaller, less massive objects like people and balls. In turn, the Sun attracts Earth.

We all learn to live with gravity from the moment we are born. Building techniques are based on people's experience with gravity and with engineering, which uses mathematical formulas to figure the materials that can be used in construction, based on their strength. As you build with blocks and other construction toys, consider how gravity determines what you can build.

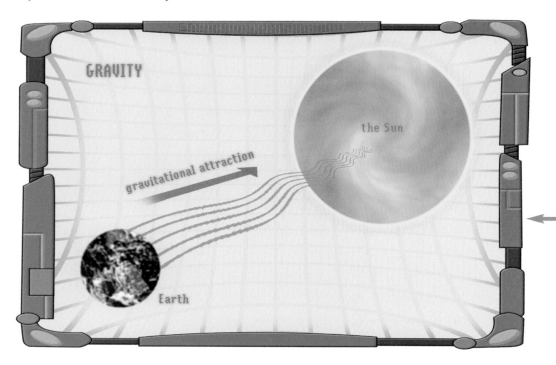

GRAVITY

the Sun

gravitational attraction

Earth

Experiments

ARCHES AND SPIRALS Brittany, Ali, and Nicole thought it might be fun to build an arch using Kapla blocks. Ali didn't think it would work. Brittany was pretty sure she could build an arch with these blocks. Nicole agreed. Each of the girls began to construct an arch. As they worked, they shared ideas on how best to stack the blocks. In the end, they had all built arches of the same shape and size.

Next, they experimented with making a spiral tower. They discovered that if they stacked the blocks carefully, they could build one. How high a tower could they build? After several attempts, they were able to create a spire of 97 blocks. They thought about the importance of the size of the base and problems with balancing. Do you have any ideas about how to build a towering tower of blocks? How high could you build it?

ROLLING TOWERS How high can you build a tower that can be moved without tumbling over? wondered Carroll, Nick, and Alex. Using Mega Bloks, they constructed a tower that was 2 blocks wide, 8 blocks long, and 46 blocks high. They placed this tower atop a block with four wheels. When they gave it a push, the whole thing toppled over like a skyscraper during a mammoth earthquake. They rebuilt it twice, but each time they pushed it, the tower toppled.

Next, the boys decided to shorten the height of the tower and see how it would work when it was made with fewer blocks. Here are their results:

39 blocks	fell after 6 pushes
29 blocks	fell after 3 pushes
23 blocks	fell after 5 pushes
18 blocks	fell after 7 pushes

They concluded that the shorter the tower, the more stable it is when moved. And the taller the tower is, the harder it is to balance. Do you think their data supports that conclusion? What else do you think might affect when the tower falls?

Some engineers have actually designed skyscrapers on wheels that are meant to roll slightly when there is an earthquake. What do you think it would it be like to be on the top floor when a big quake hits?

FAST RAMPS Does a car go farther if the ramp is steeper? Both Kyle and Rhyen predicted that a car would travel the greatest distance when it was released from the steepest ramp. Using ramps made from pipe insulation, Kyle and Rhyen sent toy cars zooming downhill. They measured the angle between the ramp and the floor with a protractor, and they used a meter stick to measure the distance the car rolled. Here are their results:

RAMP ANGLE	DISTANCE
62°	60 cm
45°	99 cm
20°	42 cm
5°	28 cm

The car flipped at the steepest angle, 62°, which prevented it from going very far. As you can see, at 45° the ramp was not so steep that the car flipped, but it was steep enough that the car went fast and far. Can you think of any ways to keep the car from flipping on the 62° ramp?

HISTORY OF BUILDING TOYS

It was the mid-1800s when simple wooden building blocks were first used in kindergartens. The famous architect Frank Lloyd Wright said he owed his interest in architecture to the blocks his mother gave to him. Wright's son, John, played with blocks, too. John became an architect whose hobby was designing building toys. In 1916 he came up with the idea of little building logs, which later became the Lincoln Logs still sold today.

A few years earlier, in 1913, a tombstone cutter named Charles Pajeau saw some children playing with pencils and empty thread spools. Their play inspired him to create a set of spools and rods called Tinkertoys.

With the invention of plastic, it wasn't long before new building toys appeared. In 1949, Ole Kirk Christiansen and his son Gotfried created Lego blocks. At first these Danish toy makers called Lego blocks "automatic binding blocks." Within a decade, kids all over the world were playing with these colorful little blocks. These days Lego makes about 11 billion blocks a year—almost enough to build a real town!

SPINNING, TURNING, AND STOPPING

There are all sorts of ways to explore the effects of spinning and turning, whether you are playing crack-the-whip or tag or toying about with a yo-yo. Like a cyclone, these whirly investigations may send you on a collision course with some scientific principles of motion. Hang on tight and enjoy the ride.

Here's a short list of some toys you could use for motion research:

- ► Foxtail
- ► gyroscope
- ► pull toy

- ► remote control car
- ► top
- ► yo-yo

HOW TO MAKE A TOP

SUPPLIES

plastic lid (from a cream cheese container)

sharpened pencil

knife

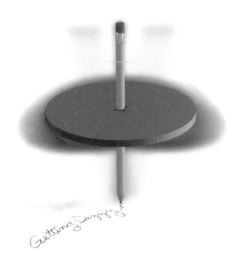

Getting Dizzy!

1. With help from an adult, cut a small cross about 1 cm each way in the very center of the lid.

2. Insert the pencil and spin the top on the point of the pencil. Adjust the lid's position on the pencil until your top spins easily.

What's the Big Idea?

OBJECTS IN MOTION Most likely you've found yourself thrown about inside a car when the driver takes a sharp turn or goes too fast around a curve. Perhaps you've experienced the value of seat belts when the car you've been in has come to a very quick stop.

As things move around, they are influenced by the forces that make them go and by the forces that make them slow down. If a car takes a curve too fast, it may actually rise up on the two inside wheels. When you are in a car that's going around a curve, the force of velocity, or speed, keeps you moving forward. Your body tries to continue in a straight path, but the car is turning toward the inside of the curve. So it feels like you are being thrown outward. This imaginary, outward-fleeing force is called centrifugal force.

CENTRIFUGAL FORCE

movement of car

momentum

imaginary
outward
force

When a car comes to a sudden halt, passengers are thrown forward because there is no force being applied to slow them down until they are held back by the seat belt. Inertia is the tendency of matter to resist speeding up or any other change in speed, such as stopping entirely. The bigger the object, the more inertia it has, and the more force must be used to start moving it or to stop it. That's why it takes so much time to stop or start something as big as a battleship.

KID Experiments

A TWIRLING BALLERINA As Jamie was fooling around with a top, she noticed how it bumped into and bounced off things, like a twirling ballerina running into walls. She placed some large washers flat on the table and watched as the top hit them. Could she make a top go through a maze?

Jamie built a wall of washers and watched as the spinning top edged along these walls. Using the washers, she made a long alley. She spun the top at the alley entrance. Once it hit the first washer, the top usually continued to spin along the washer walls.

Jamie added a turn to the alley so that it had a corner like those in a maze. To her amazement, the spinning top followed the washer wall. When it came to the corner, it turned and continued to follow the wall before it finally flopped over.

In a series of 10 more trials, the top went around the corner two more times. The other eight times, it fell over before it made it to the corner. Jamie thought that if the top would keep spinning longer, it might be able to go through a maze.

SHARP CURVES AND SHORT STOPS There really wasn't a seat for the green plastic army soldier to sit in, but Rico and Nick found a place for him to rest on the top of Rico's remote control car. Unfortunately the soldier didn't have a seat belt. Fortunately he couldn't feel a thing.

When the car sped down a big hill, the soldier stayed put. When it went around sharp turns, he just fell off. But when the car crashed into a large rock, the toy soldier went flying. The boys thought it was fun to watch him sail off the car on impact with the rock, so they repeated the

test to see how far he could go. Sometimes the toy soldier flew into the rock, but other times he flew over it. The farthest he went was about 20 centimeters. Rico and Nick wondered why the toy soldier just fell off on curves, but flew off when there was a crash. Do you have any ideas?

HISTORY OF THE YO-YO

Yo-yo is a Tagalog word. Tagalog is a native language of the Philippines, and the first yo-yos were used there over five hundred years ago. Instead of being toys, they were actually hunting tools. Hunters tossed them at the legs of animals to trip them and make them easier to kill. An American named Donald Duncan, traveling in the Philippines in the 1920s, witnessed the yo-yo in action. He realized it would make a great toy. Soon he created a smaller version, keeping the name. The company that he founded now makes yo-yos of all styles, except for hunting models!

SPACE TOYS

In space, astronauts appear to be weightless. As they float around inside or outside the spacecraft, everything that is not attached by a strap or a clip drifts away. Simple tasks, such as tightening a screw or going to the bathroom, can be very big challenges because matter acts differently on an orbiting spacecraft than it does on Earth.

On Earth, gravity holds everything down. As babies, we explore gravity by picking up and dropping objects. Imagine a baby raised on a space station and the surprise she would have if she came to Earth. Gravity's pull on everything would seem strange indeed.

What's odd about space travel is that gravity still exists, but because orbiting spaceships are moving around Earth at such a fast speed (28,000 km/h), objects in the craft end up floating. Have you ever felt weightless as you've glided back and forth on a playground swing?

After you reach the highest point and begin to fall, you are like an astronaut dropping through space. The difference between you and astronauts is that they are constantly falling. An orbiting spacecraft is falling toward Earth as it orbits, but it is zooming at such a high speed that the ball-like Earth curves away from the spacecraft as it falls. Its horizontal speed keeps it in orbit. Being in orbit on a shuttle or space station is like being on a constantly falling swing. Astronauts call this condition of apparent weightlessness microgravity, but a more accurate term is free fall.

How does free fall affect the behavior of everyday objects? What if kids lived in space? What would life be like for them?

In the mid-1980s, Dr. Carolyn Summers of the Houston Museum of Science came up with a wild and brilliant idea. Why not send toys into space? Working with the Johnson Space Center, she helped select eleven toys to send into orbit with five astronauts on the space shuttle *Discovery*. Along with the toys went questions from kids and teachers and a video camera to film the toys in action. In 1993, another set of toys blasted off in the STS-54 mission. Like kids, the astronauts had a lot of fun toying around.

One toy, a little plastic mouse that did back flips by pushing off with its feet, was nicknamed Rat Stuff. In space, Rat Stuff couldn't stick to a flat surface long enough to push off. Astronaut Don Williams tried to get Rat Stuff's feet to stick by applying hand cream to its soles. He had to add more and more until he discovered that a layer as thick as cake icing would keep Rat Stuff down long enough to jump. Later, Velcro was used to keep Rat Stuff down. Astronaut Susan Helms held Rat Stuff in her hand and pushed up as the toy pushed off with its feet. In all three instances, Rat Stuff went upward and flipped backward as he did on Earth. However, instead of landing on his feet as usual, he just continued to glide through the air.

Astronaut Jeff Hoffman had so much fun playing with magnetic marbles that he could have played with them all day. The marbles floated in rings. Chains of marbles could be swung around like kids playing crack-the-whip. As the speed of the whip increased, the centrifugal force became stronger than the magnetic attraction. Eventually the chain broke and the marbles shot off as a group in a straight line. Where do you think the chain broke? Students had thought that the last marble would fly off like in crack-the-whip, but the chain of marbles always detached from the first link.

When you spin a quarter or a top, it eventually wobbles and then clatters to a stop. What do you think tops do in space? Commander Bobko discovered that tops drift up and rotate through the air. When touched, they tilt sideways but don't totter like they do on Earth. They also spin longer.

Perhaps one day you'll have a chance to play with toys in space or watch your children or grandchildren learning what toys do while they orbit Earth.

Glossary

airfoil: the surface of a wing designed to direct the flow of air to enable flight

centrifugal force: the imaginary force that seems to make objects move away from the center of a circular path

free fall: the feeling of apparent weightlessness when an object falls continually

gravity: the force of attraction acting between objects because of their mass

inertia: the tendency of objects to stay at rest or to continue to move at a constant speed

lift: the aerodynamic force acting on a wing that causes it to rise

longitudinal waves: waves whose movement is parallel to the source of movement

matter: anything that takes up space

transverse waves: waves whose movement is perpendicular to the source of movement

velocity: speed

Metric Conversion Table

When you know:	Multiply by:	To find:
centimeters (cm)	0.394	inches (in.)
meters (m)	3.281	feet (ft.)
kilometers per hour (km/h)	0.621	miles per hour (mph)
hectares (ha)	2.471	acres
milliliters (ml)	0.2	teaspoons (tsp.)
milliliters (ml)	0.004	cups (c.)
liters (l)	1.057	quarts (qt.)
grams (g)	0.035	ounces (oz.)

To convert degrees Celsius (°C) to degrees Fahrenheit (°F), multiply by 9 and divide by 5, then add 32.

Index